PLUTONIUM & PLATINUM BLONDE

Angela M. Brommel

—
Serving House Books

Copyright 2018 by Angela M. Brommel
All rights reserved.

No part of this book may be used or reproduced in any manner whatsoever without the prior written permission of the copyright holder except for brief quotations in critical articles or reviews.

Printed in the United States of America
First Edition

Cover art and design by Jo Meuris.

ISBN 978-1-947175-01-3

Published by Serving House Books, LLC
Florham Park, NJ and Copenhagen, Denmark

www.servinghousebooks.com

This book is dedicated to my grandmother.
"You are my sunshine." —Sandy Brommel (1931-2016)

Contents

Chorus Girl	7
Betty Jane Writes Home to Mary Margaret	8
Miss Atomic and the Bomb	9
Too Soon to Ask	11
Love in the Time of Godzilla	12
Home Means Nevada	13
Miss Atomic	14
And the Smell of Orange Blossoms Everywhere	15
Catullus #50 Meets Godard's *Contempt*	16
Many Times I Have Lost/Found Myself in Water	17
From Highway 89	18
Gingerbread House	19
You Do Not Know Me	20
Late Fall, Early Winter	21
Breathless	22
Xeriscape	23
Tending the Yard	24
Datura	25
Wonder Woman at the Grocery	26
Miss Atomic at Home	27
Mojave in July	28
Catullus #7 as Her Answer from Valley of Fire	29
Lap Dance	30

Chorus Girl
—for Rovana DeBorde (1900-1954)

I.

My grandmother promised if I was good:
a cathedral wedding and a glass bottom boat.
She loved the sunny blondes; the musical blondes.
I've got the kinesthetic memory of a flapper.
Turn on Jack Benny and I channel a dead woman.

II.

My great-grandmother Rovana was a chorus girl at the Princess
Theatre. She served Jimmy Durante tea with lemon, collected
cocktail rings, stagehands—boyfriends. She tried.

She was disowned for trying too much. She tried college.
She tried modeling at the art school, wartime spot welding,
tutoring and afterschool arts. She tried marriage and babies.

III.

I was the co-ed who instigated semi-nude cartwheels
in moonlit parks, an October jump into a library's
fountain—and a few other public fountains and pools. Most likely
to kiss some boy with a bad ID who said he was nearly

an astronaut. Who missed her Movement for The Actor final
while restlessly losing her underwear in Hebron, Nebraska
during a snow storm. I tried.

I tried to start over by moving to a city of show girls.

This time I would try to be good.
This time I would try to be sunny.

I try and I try and I try, but all I want to do is play Jack Benny.

Betty Jane Writes Home to Mary Margaret

All that fussing, yards and yards of white cotton and lace,
like we hadn't done it in the backseat of his car the minute that ring
hit my finger. Then I said to him,

I've never done this before

(without rum & coke & music & a curfew).
Then he was a man and I was a wife.

Mary, have you heard about Nevada divorce ranches?
We drove from Idaho Falls to Tule Springs.
For six weeks I swam at the pool,
drank little drinks beneath the cottonwoods
while he stayed who knows where.

Let me do this one last thing for you, I said.

I hated Home Ec. Who wants to sew or iron?
I loosened every goddamn button and hem on his clothes.
Just so he'd remember me.

Miss Atomic and the Bomb

It was light in the dark
    when I whispered to him,

I want to die.
                  He pretended to sleep.

I shook and wheezed
    like a wind-up top.

Still he did nothing.

From the floodlight in the neighbors' backyard
    the light pushed through the blinds.

Illuminated   most perfect
most holy.   I had never loved him more.

                I pushed the red button.

In the bathroom covered in light
    I bit the towel to hold the scream.

It was my first time with mass destruction.
            Then the brightest whiteness,
                    the silent shattering.

Shards of glass everywhere
    something unexpected still remains
           (left side, tethered to the heart).

As an observer I thought,
    This time I have really done it.

I stepped across the circle from   Here
    to   There.

Sliding beneath the covers,
    he could only say,

Baby, let's go get a milkshake.

Too Soon to Ask

We still rely too much on the moon,
        the sound of the tree branches against the house,
the night blooming flowers.

At night when every sudden movement
        sounds like a song: The everyday is mistaken
for extraordinary, but it is much too soon to ask

where this is going. The patio is the most dangerous place
        for conversation. Beneath the awning there is the mistaken sense
that these things will save us:

Moon, privet, pomegranate, jasmine. Here we speak too soon,
        too bold. The garden with its dark warmth, and the scent
of honey smelling petals,

of white flowers caught in the blades of the overhead fan.
        Still pushing the late summer heat across the backyard as we sit
as still as stillness can, the faint sound of bad timing.

Love in the Time of Godzilla

Sometimes we are running, and I don't know where we began or where we are going. It's just a flash of trees and the cobblestone road of our favorite neighborhood where we first fell in love. We run up sidewalks and struggle with locked doors, and then just keep running as the clouds get lower and the sky turns darker. We are so used to running parallel like two multi-colored ribbons that sometimes flow over and under until they change sides and pick up again, that we don't even see each other until we pause one moment. Crouched in the peony bushes next to an old stucco house, you say she crushed you. You say the last one *really* crushed you when she walked away. I can hear the pads of heavy feet cracking the pavement only blocks away, but I just look at you and say, I can't believe that after all of these years you still complain about other women when I am the one always running with you from Godzilla. He said nothing, but his breath smelled of bitter almonds.

Home Means Nevada

You leave home for adventure,
but the highway West still knows East.

You sing 2,000 miles of *Tapestry*
and *Blue* with a guitar you cannot play.

You rename Heartache as Quest.
Endless sunshine on your windshield.

The darkness of mid-December dims
for dreamless sleep in a land of neon.

Miss Atomic

Mama, I'm a bomb
-shell. The world wants
to blow me up! A showgirl,
a bathing suit beauty.
Poolside at the casino
tourists sit and wait
wearing sunglasses, sipping
cocktails with little umbrellas
red   yellow   orange   blue
green   monkeys hanging
from the glass.   Tips are good.
Oh, what an open mouth
and a wink can do.

And the Smell of Orange Blossoms Everywhere
—after Leonora Carrington's Portrait of Max Ernst, *1939*

In Antarctica our love
is magic and metonymy.
Red striped, yellow footed bird.

Sirens & rubble.

It was an unreasonably cold summer
in this memory ball. Snow globe
of our standing still.

Exhale.

The White Horse. Glitter.

Catullus #50 Meets Godard's *Contempt*

Youth positions a girl like Bardot
ass up, questioning if truly he loves
all of her. At twenty-two this charm
captivates his wit.

She squeals through wine by the case.
On her back he traces, an alternating game
of brush and linger until the plaster falls
from the ceiling below.

She is feral beneath so much cotton.
Moonlight. If day light was near
with a chance just to speak with him.

Food ceases to taste good alone.
There is no solace in sleeping alone.

There is a deadness that rises as she reclines
on the sofa to write a poem for him.
There is a joy in suffering so deeply.

Many Times I Have Lost/Found Myself in Water

    By moonlight

Man becomes a merman.

A lonely sea creature.

Melancholy is my best seduction.

Rising from blue sheets. Each night

transpersonal, again.

Breasts, Blood, Laughter, and Fear.

On Tuesdays you draw the bath.

From Highway 89

the land looks deceptively soft with pale grasses, but as far
as you can see there is nowhere to rest. Fallen, faded stalks
of grasses have baked like unbaled hay. Now you see each blade
is a beautiful, brittle illusion of home.

Still it sways in the wind.

All around is sage, and what you want is wet black dirt,
the Kentucky Bluegrass, smell of lust that rises up
from the backyard in June. There, the Mississippi swells
underground until you can taste the water just beneath the soil.

Your hope swings like a divining rod.
The desert poppy has thorns.

Gingerbread House

I have nothing to give you but this gingerbread heart.
It is the last good cookie of my youth.

Give it to me spicy: Blackstrap molasses & a dash of white pepper
—unexpected.   Take it.   Here we are: the last glass of milk.

You Do Not Know Me
   —*after* Last Year at Marienbad

I walk a corridor with a man at each end.
One says nothing, but kills me daily with that look—always
that look. I think I muted him one too many times with a heel
to the jugular, all the while crying for freedom and a California closet.

And oh, the other man, he does not know me at all.
When he realizes he cannot ever know me—he just creates.
Montage: stockings, garter, Chanel, a boudoir.
Clutching a well-worn photograph, he took he says,

I am here with you, in this room. Replay the scene once more:
Feathers, cloak, pistol, frame after frame—and the H.O.A.
still nags about the topiaries. From far away my voice replies,
You do not know me. The trees cast no shadows.

Late Fall, Early Winter

You do not love all of the trees
that surround the yard, and often think about what it would take
to remove them, replace them, and all of the H.O.A. paperwork.

One night you go out long after the sun is gone,
cutting away so many branches of the Winter Berry.
It was not planned, you did not choose it. You cut the branches,
shape the small shrub, trying to imagine what you wanted
in its place. It will never be an English rose, and with one on each side
of the bed, it frames this: Sometimes the life of our own making,
is not of our own choosing, and yet it is what it is.

The Winter Berry belongs to the birds, and the birds were here
first. The Evening Dove, the quail, the finch, and hummingbird
are unconcerned with your understanding that landscaping is a sister
art to painting or that what you dig up at midnight is not secret.

Here you are in the middle of the night digging under a full moon
trying not to think about the berries on the shrub
you did not want, and what if you were wrong.

Breathless

Never Ingrid.
If he whistled Bogie, I whispered Bacall. *Put your lips together and blow.*

Tangerine glow
Dreamily disconnected from the subtext.
Past lights—

test sites. Pink silk
garter, stockings, head turned sideways—watching
Godard

Impossibly hard
dialogue, mostly stage business: yes   no   yes   yes.   You heart-thief.

Xeriscape

After the crab grass, the yellow oleander,
the dying cypress and endless red dirt have gone
crape myrtle, flowering plum, and bay laurel
surrounded by champagne rocks, a pathway
to a dry gray-blue river bed shaped like a heart
        or even deeper still, gardenia.

Sighing into sun-warmed rocks to think,
surrounded by spanish lavender and sweet broom
pink hawthorne, star of jasmine and rosemary
unexpectedly, delicately, silver cloud sage frames the porch
        bringing one lone hummingbird closer.

Tending the Yard

I didn't choose the Plum trees.
        That first year they didn't have the sense
to not bear fruit. We didn't have the sense to feel blessed.

How we picked each plum
        prematurely in hope
of keeping everything in order according to plan.

Such attention to detail.
        It must be baby and pet friendly. It must be
safe. It must not be more

than we can handle. I thought
        the new yard would change us. It would give
us a hobby. It would lead to a backyard wedding.

When the landscapers finished
        the dry riverbed looked like the Immaculate Heart.
It was the envy of the neighbors.

Datura

Through the window, cast the half-truth of a memory, not at all like it had been, but shaded with the regret of now. It was the night-blooming vespertine, unremarkable by day that in a few short hours by moonlight will be called marvelous. How peculiar at first, the unrecognizable sight of one's hand, the frenetic fingers of a failing gesture. A body no longer one's own. A body no longer the other's. Down in the very weeds of it all, sprawling billows of white, innocuous seeming blooms at the feet of the pomegranate tree. Had there been no song in the garden, had there been no light across your face, there would be no tomorrow.

Wonder Woman at the Grocery

Last night, in the last aisle
trapped between the unbleached
recycled toilet paper and the quilted,
bleached, twice as thick,
I waivered back and forth
imagining my eco-chicness then imagining
the actual texture of recycled toilet paper
for at least 15 minutes,
when I saw Wonder Woman.

Not even pretending to be Diana Prince,
she was pushing a cart through household goods at Smith's.
I wondered if she ever wakes up and thinks,
Today is not a good day to face the world in hot pants.
But last night she must have thought:
I save the world and I do my own shopping.

I watched her reading labels.
I wondered if Steve ever did the shopping. I wondered
if Superman ever did the shopping. But most of all I wondered
what's so wonderful about being Wonder Woman.

Miss Atomic at Home

She was a bomb

-shell. A Copa girl.

Not the first girl, no. In a series

of just right pearl-toothed, healthy

girls to make you warm at night in the desert cold,

cold war of the McCarthy right.

These girls were smart

bombs, cool blondes, Hollywood good

girls. The kind you bring home to mom

after a long day of blowing shit up. Who serves your Manhattan

with a wink, and sits on your lap while you tell her all the ways to

kill the Soviets. Not a girl who watches movies

with Commie actors. No!

A girl who does it for her country. God, country, family

and the atomic

cocktail. The kind of girl who knows just when to drop her dress

to distract you with her bathing suit beauty. She's got timing.

When she throws her arms up in the air all of Mercury takes cover:

    Flash   Boom

White Cloud   &   Fear

Mojave in July

You can't explain to friends from home how the desert makes it
better, but you try:

Imagine a heat so dry that it presses down into the earth, releasing
its scent so that it takes on the comforting smell of clay pots
in your grandmother's kitchen when you were a child,
or your hideout under the evergreens where you used to sit for hours
smelling only the dirt, the sap, the pine.

Imagine a smell that reminds you of the kitchen on holidays: sage,
rosemary, and something you chase that is reminiscent of honey,
but feels like love.

Some people still fight it. They call the heat oppressive, they call it
unrelenting. They have not learned how to live within it.

You must learn to smell the water below the surface.

You must learn to let the heat pass through you,
warming your bones, your ligaments, and all the pieces
that you call you.

Let the heat draw out everything unneeded.
Let it put you to bed midday.
Let it make you new.

Catullus #7 as Her Answer from Valley of Fire

How many of my kisses
would it take to satisfy you, you ask
as your mouth grazes the back of my knee.
As many as the grains of Mojave sand
that lie between the basin and range,
national parks, and a tiny cabin in Searchlight,
in the sun scorched canyon near the hot springs,
and in the fire-kissed valley of the petroglyphs at dusk,
or in the discarded clothes in a two-person tent
with instant soup and a game of dirty Yahtzee.
As many as these grains of sand
dance among the Joshua trees
or as many as the stars, night unmoving,
gazing down on this secret desire:
as many of your kisses, kissed
are enough, and more, for love-drunk me,
as can't be counted by exes
nor a careless word between us.

Lap Dance

Vegas taught me how to lap dance
my rage, how to take that atomic bomb
and give it to the world. The knee trick.
The hair flip. The you-can't-do-anything-
more-than-buy-me-drinks-look. The beautiful
and ugly space of desire is four miles long.
Just the good smell of vanilla and Xanadu
rolls through the air. But god
how I love the neon lights. No more
restless nights with no one else awake. Vegas gives
you color after so many drab winters.
Cold and empty is the worst way to go.
Plutonium or Platinum Blonde.

Gratitude

Within the pages of a chapbook, a slender book, I am unable to thank each of my friends and family one by one. However, I am living a life that I love because they are living it with me. I am grateful for their companionship and encouragement. I am especially grateful for my parents, Bill and Tina, and my brother, Rodney, for their unfailing love and support.

I am also grateful to have worked with extraordinary artists and writers over the years including Carol Potter, Jenny Factor, Jim Daniels, Richard Garcia, Cynthia Goatley, Vince Gotera, Tisch Jones, and Keith Reins. Special thanks to Katie Riegel, Eric Steineger, Lisa Cheby, and Telaina Eriksen for their notes on an earlier version of the manuscript.

I am grateful for the friendship and generosity of the writers, artists, arts organizations, and poetry supporters in Nevada, including my academic home for the past 14 years, Nevada State College.

I would like to thank my friend and colleague, Jo Meuris, who created the artwork and cover design for *Plutonium & Platinum Blonde*.

—

Editors Heather Lang and Timothy Lindner would like to thank Aminah Abutayeb, Madeleine Beckman, Michael Cassera, Lisa Grgas, Jo Meuris, and Risa Pappas for their dedication to this project.

Acknowledgements

I would like to thank the editors and curators of the following anthologies, art exhibitions, and journals in which these poems, or earlier versions, appeared:

"And the Smell of Orange Blossoms Everywhere," *Writers at Work LA*
"Breathless," *Now Culture*
"Catullus #7 as Her Answer from Valley of Fire," *300 Days of Sun*, *Clark: Poetry from Clark County Nevada*, and *The Best American Poetry Blog*
"Catullus #50 Meets Godard's *Contempt*," *Vapid Kitten* and *The Best American Poetry Blog*
"Datura," *Helen: A Literary Magazine*
"Chorus Girl," *North American Review*, *Clark: Poetry from Clark County Nevada*, and *Lunch Ticket Special*
"From Highway 89," *Sweet: A Literary Confection*, and *All of Us: Sweet: The First Five Years*
"Home Means Nevada," *Helen: A Literary Magazine* (awarded the 2017 Helen Stewart Poetry Award)
"Lap Dance," *The Citron Review*, *Petite Hound Press*, and *Clark: Poetry from Clark County Nevada*
"Late Fall, Early Winter," *The Red Rock Review*
"Love in the Time of Godzilla," *The Citron Review*
"Many Times I Have Lost/Found Myself in Water," *Clark: Poetry from Clark County, Nevada*
"Mohave in July," *300 Days of Sun*, *Transcribing Nevada*, *Clark: Poetry from Clark County, Nevada*.
"Miss Atomic at Home," *300 Days of Sun* and *Legs of Tumbleweeds, Wings of Lace: An Anthology of Literature by Nevada Women*
"Tending the Yard," *The Citron Review* and *The Literary Review* (TLR Share)
"Wonder Woman at the Grocery," *The Citron Review*
"Xeriscape," *The Red Rock Review*
"You Do Not Know Me," *Now Culture*

www.ingramcontent.com/pod-product-compliance
Lightning Source LLC
Chambersburg PA
CBHW061348040426
42444CB00011B/3151